GEOGRAPHY OF THE US
SOUTH REGION STATES
(TEXAS, FLORIDA, DELAWARE AND MORE)

GEOGRAPHY FOR KIDS - US STATES
5TH GRADE SOCIAL STUDIES

BABY PROFESSOR
EDUCATION KIDS

Speedy Publishing LLC
40 E. Main St. #1156
Newark, DE 19711
www.speedypublishing.com
Copyright 2017

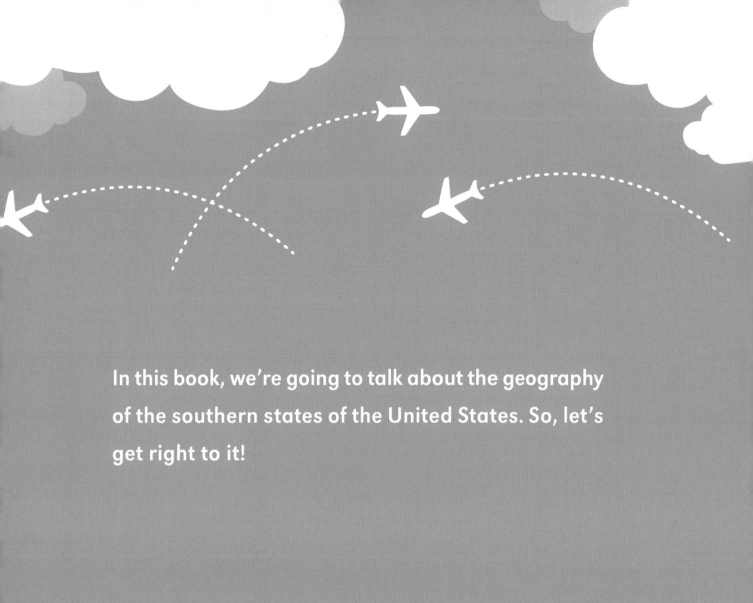

In this book, we're going to talk about the geography of the southern states of the United States. So, let's get right to it!

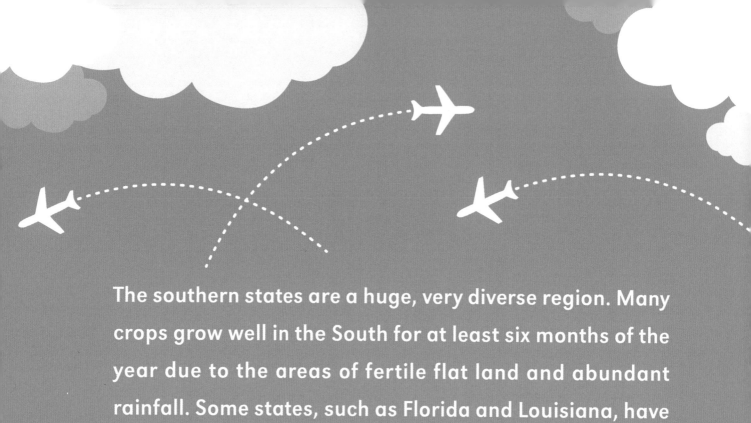

The southern states are a huge, very diverse region. Many crops grow well in the South for at least six months of the year due to the areas of fertile flat land and abundant rainfall. Some states, such as Florida and Louisiana, have extensive areas of swamps. Many of the southern states border the Gulf of Mexico or face out onto the Atlantic Ocean. There are so many states in this region that they are frequently broken down into different groups and they are not always categorized the same way. Here is one way they are frequently organized.

GULF OF MEXICO

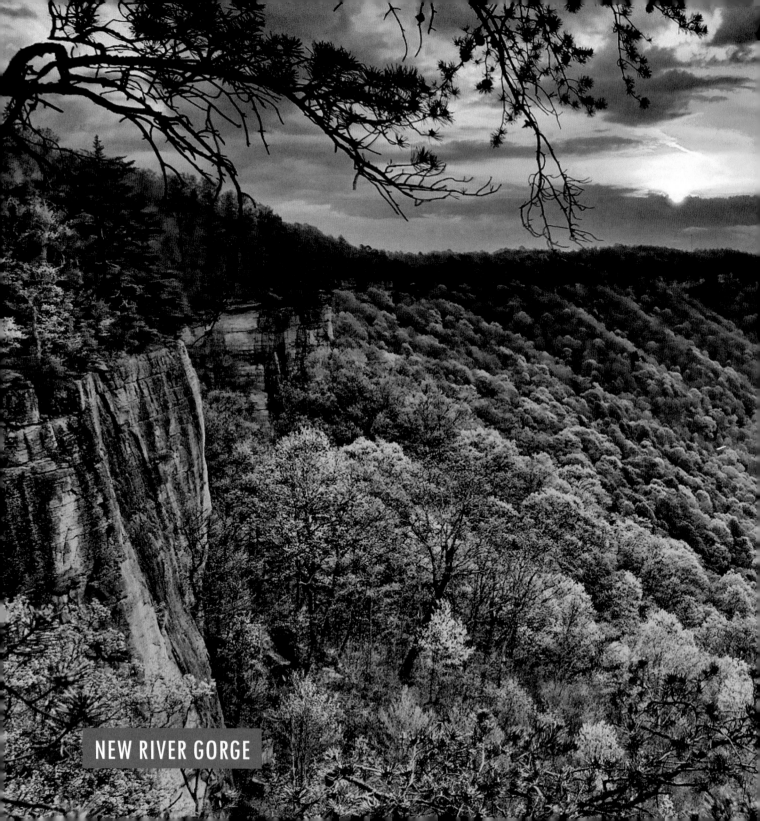

NEW RIVER GORGE

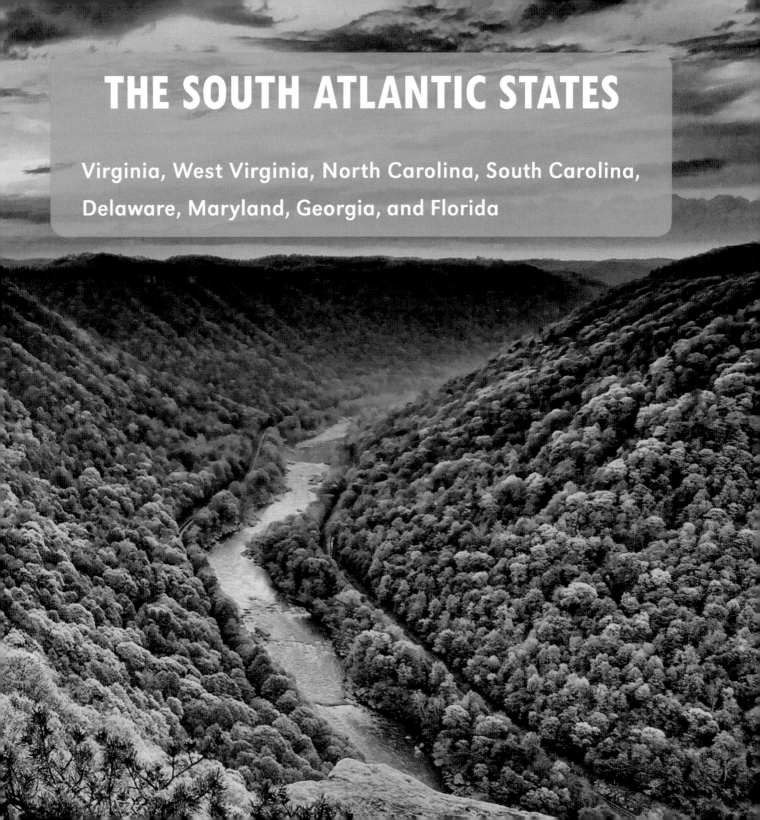

THE SOUTH ATLANTIC STATES

Virginia, West Virginia, North Carolina, South Carolina, Delaware, Maryland, Georgia, and Florida

THE EAST SOUTH CENTRAL STATES

Alabama, Kentucky, Mississippi, Tennessee

ALABAMA

BIG BEND NATIONAL PARK

THE WEST SOUTH CENTRAL STATES

Texas, Oklahoma, Arkansas, Louisiana

Here are more details about the geography of some of these states.

NEW ORLEANS, LOUISIANA

RIO GRANDE RIVER

TEXAS

Texas has five major regions. The Gulf Coastal Plain region covers the state of Texas from the Rio Grande River in the state's southwestern corner to its eastern border with the state of Louisiana. The southern section of this area has rich, fertile soil ideal for farming. A densely forested area called the Piney Woods extends into southeastern Texas from Louisiana.

West of the Gulf Coastal Plains are the Prairie Plains, which have rugged terrain with rolling hills. The Black Waxy Prairie, an area with very fertile soil, is also in this region. The Rolling Plains region continues the terrain of rolling hills into the north-central section of the state.

PRAIRIE PLAINS

GREAT PLAINS

To the west is the Great Plains region, which is a flat treeless area. It extends into the Texas panhandle. At the far western edge of the state is the Basin and Range region. The terrain there is composed of high plains interrupted by mountain ranges such as the Santiago, Davis, and Guadalupe. The highest peak is Guadalupe Peak, which has an elevation of 8,751 feet.

OKLAHOMA

Oklahoma has ten major regions, which is more than any other state.

The eastern section of the state is split between the Ozark Plateau region, which is a hilly area, and the Ouachita Mountains region in the southeast. The Prairie Plains region is wedged in between these two regions and also extends west.

OUACHITA MOUNTAINS

ARKANSAS RIVER

This is a low-lying area that includes the Arkansas River Valley. West of the Prairie Plains is an area of plains that covers most of the central portion of the state and has a gradually rising elevation. Forests cover most of this area, except where interrupted by two small mountain ranges.

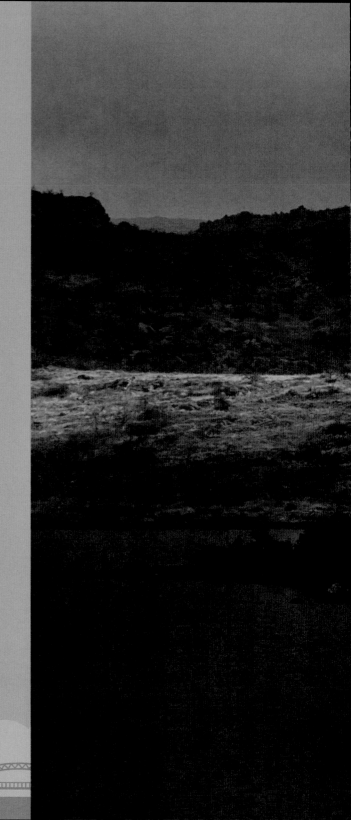

In the south-central portion of the state is the Arbuckle Mountain region and in the southwest are the Wichita Mountains. Along the state's southern border is the Red River region, which is fertile and suited to agriculture.

WICHITA MOUNTAINS

BLACK MESA

The northwestern panhandle, covered by the High Plains region, is a grassy area that has the state's highest elevations. In the northwest corner, Black Mesa rises to a height of 4,973 feet in elevation. Due east of the High Plains region is the Gypsum Hills Region. Continuing east is the Red Beds Plains region. Between the Red Beds Plains and the Prairie Plains is the Sandstone Hills Region.

ARKANSAS

Arkansas has five major regions. In the northwest section of Arkansas there are two highlands areas: The Ozark Plateau and the Ouachita Mountains.

The Ozark Plateau is densely forested and contains the Boston Mountains. South of the Ozark Plateau is the Ouachita Mountain region, which has ridges and valleys and is known for its hot springs.

BOSTON MOUNTAINS

MISSISSIPI RIVER

These two mountainous areas are divided by the Arkansas River Valley region. Although the Arkansas River Valley is a lowland, it contains several mountain peaks including Magazine Mountain, which is the highest in the state at 2,753 feet. The rest of the state is lowlands composed of the Mississippi Alluvial Plain, a fertile area fed by the Mississippi River, and the West Gulf Coastal Plain.

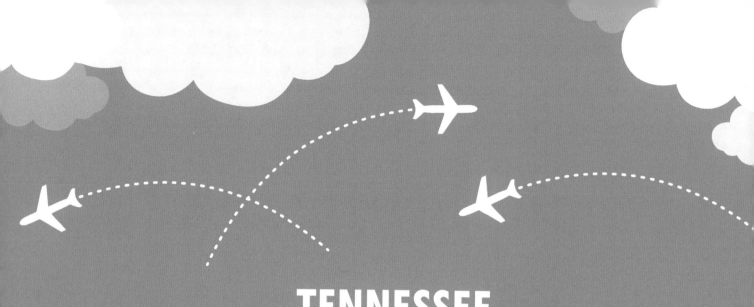

TENNESSEE

Tennessee has six major regions. The eastern border of the state lies in the Blue Ridge region, which is part of the Appalachian Mountain region. The highest elevations in the state, including Clingmans Dome, which is 6,643 feet, are found there. The Great Smoky and Bald Mountains are also in this region.

APPALACHIAN MOUNTAINS

APPALACHIAN RIDGE AND VALLEY

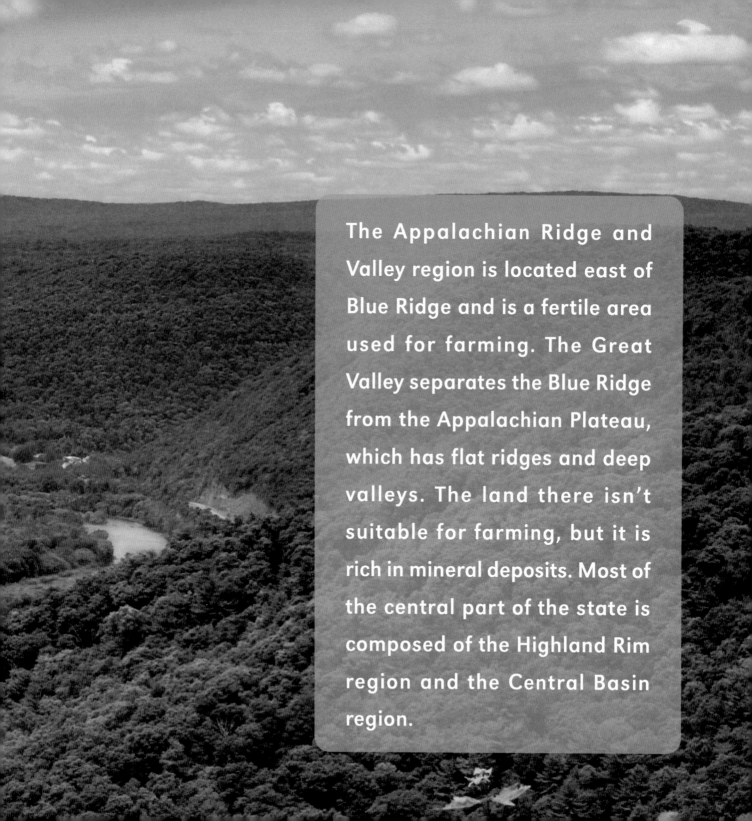

The Appalachian Ridge and Valley region is located east of Blue Ridge and is a fertile area used for farming. The Great Valley separates the Blue Ridge from the Appalachian Plateau, which has flat ridges and deep valleys. The land there isn't suitable for farming, but it is rich in mineral deposits. Most of the central part of the state is composed of the Highland Rim region and the Central Basin region.

The Central Basin is made of gentle hills with fertile soil for agriculture. The Highland Rim surrounds the Central Basin. It is a flat plain at a higher elevation than the Basin. Along Tennessee's western border is the Gulf Coastal Plain region, which extends up from the Gulf of Mexico.

GULD COASTAL PLAINS

APPALACHIAN

GEORGIA

Georgia has five major regions. The northern part of Georgia is divided into two mountain ranges. In its northwest corner is the Appalachian Plateau region where mountains are interspersed with fertile valleys of the Appalachian Ridge and Valley region.

East of this region is the southernmost section of the Blue Ridge Mountain region. These mountains contain the highest elevations in the state with some peaks over 4,000 feet.

BLUE RIDGE

APPALACHIAN

South and east of the Appalachian-Blue Ridge Range is the Piedmont region, which slopes in a south direction from an elevation of 2,000 feet to a lower elevation of 300 feet. This region contains major cities like Augusta and Atlanta. The southern part of the state is covered by the Coastal Plain, which is predominantly farmland except for the southeast corner that is largely covered by the Okefenokee Swamp bordering Florida.

FLORIDA

Florida has three major regions. Most of the state of Florida is composed of flat plains. The eastern part of the state is the Atlantic Coastal Plain region, which extends up the eastern coastline all the way to the state of New York. Off Florida's Atlantic coastline are a series of sandbars and barrier islands.

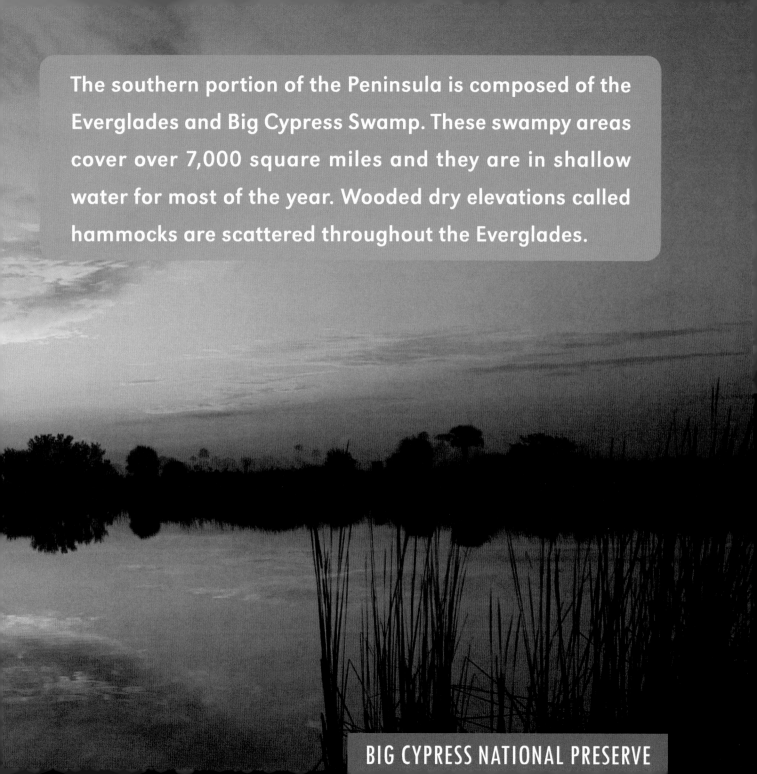

The southern portion of the Peninsula is composed of the Everglades and Big Cypress Swamp. These swampy areas cover over 7,000 square miles and they are in shallow water for most of the year. Wooded dry elevations called hammocks are scattered throughout the Everglades.

BIG CYPRESS NATIONAL PRESERVE

The Florida Keys are a string of islands that curve southwest off the Florida coast. They are the southernmost point of the continental United States. The East Gulf Coast Plain on Florida's western shore faces toward the Gulf of Mexico. Much of the Florida panhandle is a higher elevation than the rest of the state, but none of it rises more than 300 feet above sea level. This region of low hills is known as the Florida Uplands.

CYPRESS SWAMP

DELAWARE

The state of Delaware only has two different regions. Most of the state is in the Atlantic Coastal Plain that extends along most of the east coast from Florida to New York. This area is mainly flatlands with low hills and pastures. In the southern section of the state there are marshlands, including the Cypress Swamp in the southernmost part of the state. The Cypress Swamp covers more than 25,000 acres of land. Surprisingly, Delaware has the lowest mean elevation in the United States at 60 feet.

In the northeast corner of the state is a small section called the Piedmont region. This region has gentle hills and valleys of rich farmland that stretch as far south as the state of Alabama. The highest elevation in the state at only 442 feet is found there, close to the border next to Pennsylvania and Maryland.

PIEDMONT

CHESAPEAKE BAY, EASTERN SHORE, VIRGINIA

VIRGINIA

Virginia has five major regions. The eastern part of the state is located in the Atlantic Coastal Plain region, which is also known as Tidewater. This region is a low-lying flat area that goes from the Atlantic coastline inland about 100 miles. The terrain there is divided up by several rivers.

There are also several swamp areas including the Dismal Swamp, which is located in the southeast. The central part of the state is the Piedmont region. It has gently rolling hills that gradually slope to about 1000 feet in elevation at the foot of the Blue Ridge Mountain region. The northwestern part of the state belongs to the Appalachian Plateau and Appalachian Ridge and Valley regions.

GREAT DISMAL SWAMP

GULF OF MEXICO

SUMMARY

The geography of the South is very diverse and is composed of mountains, hilly terrain, grasslands, fertile farming areas, and large areas of swamp. Due to their location, the southern states have a long growing season. Many of the southern states have coastlines either along the Gulf of Mexico or along the Atlantic Ocean. The southern state of Florida has coastlines along both.

Awesome! Now that you've read about the geography of the South section of the United States, you may want to read about the geography of the Midwest in the Baby Professor book Geography of the US – Midwest States (Illinois, Indiana, Michigan, Ohio and More) | Geography for Kids – US States.

Made in the USA
Coppell, TX
26 September 2021